Riding Untouched

RIDING UNTOUCHED

Timothy Houghton

ORCHISES

Washington

1998

Library of Congress Cataloging in Publication Data

Houghton, Timothy, 1955-
   Riding untouched / Timothy Houghton
       p.   cm.
     ISBN 0-914061-68-2 (alk. paper)
     I. Title.
   PS3558.0848R53   1998
   813'.54—dc21   97-29715
                                                                CIP

ACKNOWLEDGEMENTS

Some of these poems appeared in the following magazines: *American Literary Review*, *Birmingham Poetry Review*, *California State Poetry Quarterly*, *Chelsea*, *Cimarron Review*, *College English*, *Confrontation*, *Dominion Review*, *Hayden's Ferry Review*, *Literary Review*, *Midland Review*, *Poet Lore*, *Tar River Poetry*, *Widener Review*, and *Wisconsin Review*.

"The Remaining Warmth" and "Sanctuary" appeared in *Lilt,* an annual art/poetry anthology from Kansas City Art Institute.

I wish to express my gratitude to the Corporation of Yaddo, the Djerassi Program, the Ragdale Foundation, the Virginia Center for the Creative Arts, and the Helene Wurlitzer Foundation for fellowships allowing me to work on these poems.

Special thanks to my wife, Cindy Moore, for her support and advice.

ORCHISES PRESS
P. O. Box 20602
Alexandria
Virginia
22320-1602

for all my family,

especially Bill

CONTENTS

I

First Day of School

They seem so strange from here—
the coins we spun on desktops,

trying to spot the presidents
who floated in whimsical orbits,

in turbulent, spinning globes
of air and clouds. Crouched low

I could see through them
to the other side of the desk

where a kid's eye out of nowhere
might be looking at mine

across the desert. Our quarters especially
exulted in conflict

even as they clanged and staggered
into a weighty silence—

but roving among them all
were the limber, secretive dimes,

my favorites, the spies
who reported the plots and carnage

if they escaped unfallen
to my thumb and finger.

I remember holding one in my pocket
after the first bell rang,

after we sat at our desks
and saw the teacher

touch the clock on the wall
and begin the explanation of time.

Riding Untouched

It was hour-old rain
drawing up the shine in benches,

springing the green algae
and scale of greys

from rotting boards. The slow overcast
added density

to the peace of black bark
in legions of trees. Those benches—

at odd angles to the path, awry
from years of backs

and legs stretching out—
combined with the woods

to remind me of a room
with huge French doors

where the black dinner table
and black chairs

stood higher than me. Beneath them
I fought my brothers

among the trolls
and visored knights of that era,

flailing my weapons, riding untouched
between the riddled trees.

Sanctuary

Sometimes during visits
we see our mother pretending to bustle

in the quiet of her old bedroom
that's used for storage now—

where she's kept the windows
swollen shut for over thirty years

for fear that *loosening them
will break the glass.* The unwashed panes

are giant laboratory slides
preserving a soup of grit and oils

from children's fingertips:
a history of touches

between herself and the birches
which line our street. The whole warmth

of sunlight coming free of a cloud
and coming in—not here. Lately

my brothers and I discovered
one of our father's coats

still hanging in the closet
and stood there trading memories

of seeing different aspects of him
in that herring-bone brown.

This means we've stopped teasing her
about the room. We keep quiet.

Home Movie

Like a burlap sack
filled with implements

she's no-nonsense, my great-aunt
leaving the henhouse

but laughing with all of us here
when my parents play it

backwards. She opens a hand
I know is soft

and fat with wrinkles, presenting
two smooth eggs

before returning
to the smell of feathers and straw,

the egg-beds behind
the warped wooden door. Nearly

forty years ago
we watched that blind

ungainly walk, and many times
I've wanted to go back:

the unmistakable
ticking of the projector's time,

the dark room
and living family then, the chair

warmer than this one now,
and a curtain

dreaming against the outside light
I want to keep out.

Between Fields

Maybe he'll run on the gravel road
near the house where he grew up.

No sound of trucks
and no one's watching, though he glances twice

at the open loft
of a neighbor's barn. He takes time

to examine the firmness of shadow
throughout the air—something to do with sweat

cooling on his shirt, with roadside trees
blocking the hot sun

at three o'clock. Those flashes of blue
going tree to tree

are indigo buntings
helping settle his return to the early days

and gird his desire to run
and test the gravel, the dense air—to run as he did

when trying to beat the throw,
when one guy held the ball and counted to four

before flinging it to a kid
ninety feet away. But too much here is the same,

the road more successful than he'd like
in its shifting of tense—

seeming just too big
with memories. He smells the hedge-apples again

and grabs one to throw. . .
but turns it instead, inspects it,

tosses it up and down in his hand
with hard focus, as though it's heavier now,

as though it's inconceivable his large hand
can hold it.

The Fireflies

Looming with gutters
and ghost-lit from windows inside,

the walls seemed high as a fort
when I followed my father

around our house
until we stopped out back. He said *look*

and pointed at the northern lights
which covered a hole in crowded treetops,

lights that maneuvered in wavy bursts
like a confident army

in regions of forest. Years later
above tree line in the Absarokas

the songs of hidden birds
were spreading their questions overhead

and moments after seemed to fall
down walls of a cirque—as if to protect

its ancient reliquary. A rat skeleton
took a corner of the cellar

in my childhood home—an unruly grid
against the dirt floor,

it stayed as a joke, my father knowing
he'd keep seeing the wonder

in my eyes. Out walking last night
when dozens of fireflies

were probing the rough line of branches
where the boulevard

turns back from the woods—it was then
I remembered his gift.

Winter Feeder

Each morning, stiff in the minus weather
I filled the tube near a lilac

whose complication of twigs, of loops
and knots, surrounded the waiting birds:

a stark and leafless roominess
that seemed to embody their hunger

and puzzled the sky behind it.
I was happy when time stopped behaving

the morning I offered a handful of seed—
the goods of energy and instinct,

of maybe a warmer attachment too—
and walked slowly toward the feeder, careful

not to light the fireworks
in frozen leaves below.
                        I think it was sunlight

doubled by snow
that took me back for a few seconds—

to strips of sunlight on the kitchen floor
when I was too young for school,

for shoveling snow after a blizzard. Magazines
on the breakfast table

always seemed open to pictures of fall
whose trails of yellow leaves

were a mixture of warmth and near sadness
held in my mother's face

as she talked of the past.

                    I'm close now
                    and a siskin

feels like twigs on my palm
for the moment it eats, before flying.

After School

There'd been a circle,
a choker
            of clamor and teeth,

of greasy hair, white t-shirts
and jeans ripe

with dirt
and taut, skinny muscle: the kids

who surrounded my older brother
and the other guy.

                        Busted streetlights
                        fronted a blue sky,

and the nap of old t-shirts
was loud with ritual, machinery

drawing the circle
tighter—
            until adults from outside

said *Put that down!*
to the mean one
                        with the broken bottle

who obeyed—but went down himself
in that moment's
                        distraction, struck

by my brother
who took no chances,

                    who stepped hard

on his neck, until he screamed
defeat.

The Rain Between

For a short time I'd been at my desk,
fixed on trees
        densely lining
        the chain-link fence

in the back, just looking
out the window,
        not hearing or seeing the rain—

but fixed on trees where a thickness
of blackbirds
        rose like smoke
        behind the green leaves,

in the darkness of limbs and burls. I was scared
for my brother,
        his troubles
        at home and work,

and thinking of the unplanned distances
between us.
        As kids in the big space

in front of our parents' two-car garage,
we rode our bikes
        in frantic circles:

the game of *high speed,* when I'd smash him
from behind. . .
        and always the memory
        of sunlit gravel and glare

from the fenders—when all at once I noticed
the fine streaks
                    falling quietly, straight

on the tree-bordered yard: a roomful
of rain
            above the grass shining strangely
            in the grey light.

Movement in the Grass

When he touches it, the glass ball
of the nightlight

reddens his fingers. Distant eyes
frighten his mother

whose tone
follows her hand along his arm

as she tells where families
come together

after death. She wants to convince him
of future and place,

his dead father waiting
in a spirit-trick of certainty and flesh.

Hearing *son*
he flashes to a huge and fulgent yard

where both parents
are pointing at movement in the grass—

then snaps back
to a touch on hair and ear.

She leaves the door half open,
her shadow impressed in the hall

and in the slurred ticking
of a rotating fan. Specters on toy shelves

gather around him
and do what they can for his sleep.

The Unseen and Its Hills

Where the road changed
into gravel,
>we turned onto blacktop

away from the small bridge
and the river we'd been skirting.
>Up front—

my parents and the direction home,
a town's edge. "Nothing's down there"

defined the gravel stretch
I wanted to see for no clear reason

after church and a visit to old relations.

A second bridge in the distance
close enough
>to be a vulnerable secret

seemed a place for walking
with particular vision—

>its reflected traffic
>blowing crumpled and thin

like candy wrappers
across the rough water.

>There'd been a red blanket

patched with wetness,
with the unseen and its hills, its pitches

into shadow—and mention of a body
weeks before on the news.
                              None of it

quite in mind until later
except in a feeling of where to go.

Three Brothers

They've circled each other
with child-tones

all their lives, funny-talk
of insects creamed with a hammer

beside the doghouse, or the guillotine
severing basketballs

from a straw dummy. Ph.D.'s
don't matter—it's been old times

and love-bunting, early dialect
deep into age.
                    Where the mother still lives

the attic door remains unwashed
of *Scientists At Work*—

Do Not Disturb. After the death
of her husband

she kept her ear
at the bottom of the stairs—

her children absorbing
a direction
                    subtle as gloss in a margin—

and held the kingdom together

as the secret maker
of their language.

II

Their Laughter

When the hornet finally died
its blue wings—

> translucent and sturdy
> as mica—

crossed themselves and covered the body
as it lay on the sill,

and I was surprised
to find myself thinking of water,

how it comes up blue
> after wind blows away
> the floating seaweed—

when black-crowned terns
hover above fish—

> and remembered a story
> I heard from my father,

one of many troops swimming
at a Philippine beach
> as lobsters boil
> in a metal drum.

Planes come swooping low
from jungle canopy,
> strafing the diving men
> whose stomachs are filled

with white meat, and the miracle is no one
gets hit,
                    that it's one

pass only. They surface with shouts,
with fists raised

but dissolved in spindrift—and laughter,
violent laughter
                    like glare
                    and white water on the blue.

Dark Glove

It didn't take much
this time

      for muscles to clamp at brow and nape,
      for sight to go unclear

as though the space before him had prepared itself
against too much seeing—

        he'd only
        been looking outside

where even the smallest branches stayed still
while their leaves blew together

like a subtle intelligence, enticing, but for no one's
understanding. . .

when the gauzy tension took over his eyes.
It will come round, he thought—and forced a smile

when ice he took from his drink
and drew across his brow
        did nothing to stop
        the burning.

He looked out the window again
and breathed the air of something anonymous—

. . . an absence of veining in leaves.

He owned a picture in the back of his mind,
there for several years:

a dark glove
tightly gripped a balustrade

at the top of stairs
and above the glove—a smile
willed into position:

a tension of skin. He wanted to know, to draw out
the realness
of the person living then, the whole life
of one time and place—

but the effort was failing again
as glove and smile were taken into the leaves

with only the loss left, deep and vague
as the wide stairway.

Mohawk Winter

No moon lay that night
on Mohawk, but he knew the lake

and where it would hold. He went there
every night—to hear the branches

cracking, and cars passing
on the country road, the ice

catching every sound,
throwing it back to him. Here at this hour

he found where years had gone,
the ice extending forever,

smooth and pure: a black rebus
whose cold, hard faces

were felt but never seen—and one night
by accident, he kicked a piece of ice

that slid across
the undisturbed surface. When he picked it up

the sharp edges
softened in his grip. Then he touched

the surface below:
smooth, cold, hard—undisturbed.

After Bad Dreams

Joined on his chest,
his hands are structured for calm

as he lies in bed
waiting for the algal haze

to burn away
in the curtained light—yet the germ,

persistent, tunnels
like staph. He's a right-lane driver today,

but news of more trees
falling in Brazil

arrives before he can switch
to anything quiet. He feels unframed

at work—amused that coffee
trembles on his desk

when he places the receiver
after a call. Those shady characters

he woke from—their vague demands
seem to involve history,

a desired revision
of some portion he currently attends,

but the second cup
closes that book, pulling him back

from a daydream of trees, of his home
concealed among them

in a lush distance.

Under Pine Trees

Through layers of needles
sunlight reaches her body

like a dropped puzzle.
                              The old woman
                              looks into it

from a lounge chair
in the park, her eyes moving

under the uneven shade
as though seeking flight. There's blue

cut into mineral pieces—with the whole
just several stories up.

Boisterous chickadees
suggest the blinding hope of it all,

the way out
to something real,
                              kindred, and lasting.

Here the sky is sharpened to fine edges
that slip into her lungs. It's more

          than blood coursing
          under her skin

and lighting the back of her hands
late blue. She's taken

by what she sees,

the angel-signs,
the mineral pieces

of her thoughts, the language saying
let no one mourn for me.

Waiting

*. . . my body is still just good enough to enjoy the wind from the
electric fan that turns this way and that, wind on my chest, wind on
my legs, wind on my legs.*

—Max Frisch in Homo Faber

He wants wholeness
this second—

as if the snow he's gripping in a paperweight
could say more
                    than coldness and vanishing

left in his hand by real flurries. "Real"
is made of easy impressions, fractions

of the total message
whose parts go largely invented

like debris at a distance:

          prop roots of rubber
          and watery flashes from shards of glass

on old train tracks
below the viaduct

he'd taken to work just weeks ago.

. . .

The held-close memories are too mixed
with faith,
          vagueness. He'd like to call back

the sharpness of exhausted warblers in May,
the gold cap or black mask

just feet away
after a long migration.

  Two straight mornings—
   a few feathers below the window.

It's the half-dreaming time
and he draws close to the bird,
        the precision

of color, the precision of line—
no matter
   the dirty pledge of his body.

Bat

I'm thinking of the black coat

I'd worn at night
years ago when walking hard,

forcing my steps
to bring a blood to my face

that might overwhelm
the grey light of sadness.

There's a second warmth too
in the repeated pattern

of its flight,
as if it's erecting a structure

in my backyard space
where I'm walking tonight in peace,

where I'm sensing the walls
of an ancient protection

like the surviving turret
of a fortress in ruins.

Old Room

He jerks back
when his face brushes

a cobweb—unwelcome hint, pendular
movement slowing
     to near levitation

then plumb line.

    <u>I only have to move</u>
    <u>and the place comes alive.</u>

When direct sun
hits his eye through a window,

he turns quickly, taking the glare with him
to shelves of books,

their spines
glowing like travertine. He touches them

and his hands take part in the shine—
soon enough

your hands will rest against your pockets
and the musty smell of books assert itself

in memory. Whatever legacy
remains like druse in a dull stone—

draw from that river.

Your name is no anagram.
Keep the good deaths alive.

Trouble Sleeping

You think of your cells aging.
You think of plain stone
                        pinching off

a mineral thread of light and color:
no heaven
            is the blank map

making you worry. Then daily things
add up to duckboard

sinking below the mire.
                        Your wife sleeps
                        and can't help—

you may as well start digging
you're already so low to the ground—

when your images
decide on their own
                        to go a lucky route:

alpine flowers hug the ground
at an altitude

                where sky is widest
                with wind and lit-up blue.

You look so closely at what grows here

sleep must come
you're so hidden.
                        Stupid to worry.

Whatever the late birds are saying

echoes a long way, filling
the thin air around you.

Cibola

After an all-night rain
learned the crooked way through adobe

and fell near my bed,
after a dream of drownings in the street,

I had to smile
at the anger outside—my neighbors

with mud on their boots
and something to talk about. On top of the corn

sparrows announce boundaries
for hours each day, their swiveling heads

aware of threats
all around. The stalks where they sing

go into the mix
and keep the mud bricks unbroken. Only

a ghostly rain
could ferret that system of micro tunnels

and hit the floor with bad clocks
and inject my sleep

with so many deaths. But the window glares
where the rain left tracks,

admitting hints
of old worlds I learned as a kid—suggestions

of gold in the mundane energy
of voices, of engines grinding in the street,

and the morning's prompted sun.

Her Leaving

Tonight he tries reading
a novel he'd loved before

but can't bring it to wholeness,

as if distant bass notes
are thudding throughout the words,

creating dark pockets
he can't inhabit—

so he sits still and stares at the floor

because it makes the least demands,
because the flat, grey carpet

bears the compulsion of his gaze
like a frozen slick.

. . .

He shuts his eyes
and sees abstracted colors

in random gusts of firing nerves.

He finds some comfort
in their purity,

their unearthly forms
and energy—where no trees, no arms

extend in real places.

. . .

Out walking, he looks at ice
enclosing black branches

and knows what to take into sleep:

the coldness
of nival strength.

Vines he'd meant to pull
are still wedged

into cracks of siding,
and he recalls their tenacity—

how deep they've managed to go.

III

Bufo Alvarius

*(In 1991, researchers identified a toad as the first animal ever
documented to harbor an hallucinogenic agent.)*

Dizzied by heat waves, they burned a chip
of dried venom

and sucked that smoke in. What a fraught
afterbirth!—
    the word "Yes"

slowly exhaled. They saw their skin go bumpy,
alvarian,
    noting its odor of rich coffee—

and little comets salted the air, darting
at midday:
    cactus thorns. An earnest blue haze

formed a marquee
     of precious metals, a wafting
     mist distilled

from Bufo's eyes. Imagine! Dry leaves
blessed wrinkles,
     and lines on their palms

said *Death is natural. Death is good.* Their nods
finished the wisdom. With glory

poised, their names
     lit the marquee. No one
     could talk.

The Remaining Warmth

The twelve-foot fraction of tentacle
lay on the shore

like a thick whip—like a tool
used by dangerous, benthonic

orders. Children who touched it
studied their fingertips

before running from this proof
of giants, of still-living

never-seen monsters
of concealment and wonder.

At great depths
below the apprehension of light

there's a remaining warmth
where unnerving work gets done—

and slowly the good fears rise up
to be with our days

like hail banging on windshields
of moving cars

with sheets of rain
waving at us from the road ahead.

Iceman

Tall as a house, the glacial ice
crept over the rocky hole

that walled his corpse. Sometimes snow
would blow from the surface

and guerrilla light
take a staggered route

down the stories of ice—exploring veins
of the marble pendant

worn on his chest, circling the orbits
in which darkness

replaced the eyes. Now it's melted
to shreds of leather,

to skin defined by bone
and teams of science. Five thousand years

after the foehn
sucked him dry in the Alps,

the serried marks
fired into his loins with charcoal

are blue fuel
of clannish assertion. Those feathers

precisely aligned on his arrows
could still guide a killing flight.

City Mall, City Zoo

1.

With the unfiltered reaction
of fear,
the lunch crowd quickly passes

a clutch of young men
aping the walk of a woman in heels.

Unswerving eyes
are her facade

for the deep-muscled tension
and vulnerability
of her face stiffening

in response to their laughter behind her.

Gripped like darts
their cigarettes
color the aftermath,
our impotence.

2.

A bottle breaks—someone's little girl
kicks pieces of glass

into the water,
                the surfacing mouths
                of giant goldfish.

Gentle fingers tug at her shoulder strap
while her clan
                lengthen their necks

and take a curious look below
before ambling on
                to the end of the bridge

and the start of more cages.
I'm thinking about borders now

and the lack of peace on a clear afternoon

whose tropical birds
                        grip the upper mesh
                        of the aviary,

wanting, like many of us
on this average day, out.

The Volgograd Fields in Russia

*(Hitler's instructions not to surrender resulted in the death of
200,000 soldiers of the German Sixth Army.)*

The season might explain the white smears
in the distance

and suggest a final snow
melting roughly in the tough, sparse grass

where ocher-tinted soil shows itself
without effort. Or maybe the lights

are frosted remnants of whatever dew
can form on gullies and swells

of dry steppes. With cirrus clouds
scattered like lint

against it, the sky in its brilliance
seems especially remote

as, walking, we see the smears evolve slowly,
and only when we're at the first of them

are they revealed
as a litter of sun-bleached bones

on the *balki*, all the way to its horizon
in open view, where normally you'd imagine

the snow, the frost, the dew—
and glaring reflections

of melting light. Thousands of bones
just lying there, a few with gritty identity tags

between them, not far from plowed fields
where children rummage

and sometimes spark the unexploded shells
in spring thaw—some losing a foot, others dying

near the old death. Where buttons of uniforms
lie between ribs, it's hard

to close things up and explain. It's hard
to mourn where the boundary of bones

is so scattered
and so many soldiers impossible to name

except as "cadavers
of obedience"

who lie before the distant seam of trees
planted after the war, in the dry expanse.

Pontito

*(Franco Magnani lives each day with the constant occurrence of
three-dimensional apparitions of the Italian village where he lived
as a boy during the '30s and '40s. He paints the reconstructions of
those memories at his home in San Francisco.)*

Some nights the terracing takes him to sleep.
He climbs

        the old practice of farming, each step
        a phrasing of time

where olives had grown
before the war tore down

those fields and his father
who watched them.
          His answer outlines the safety

of a new land's peace
         where the stone wall
         he built around his house

is a risen current
of carved fish
        like those in Pontito's creek

before bombs made it a sprawl
of mud and rocks and fish
          dead on their sides.

Each day the holograms
reward his longing—buildings
          as real to him

as the finger he points to explain them,
the history
            of rooms and people unseen

behind invented walls—his town lit
like the pale chalk

on undersides of leaves. Friends today
know their place
            in his rapture, his focus

on the world he paints
so minute, intense,

                        they are perhaps no more
                        than degrees of shading

on masonry stones.
                        He'll never go back
                        to the dying town

he's heard about, never roll up the canvas,
take it there
            and steer his eyes between them.

Two Lives

*(In his New York City apartment where he lives with his wife and
mother, the Russian-born mathematician Gregory Chudnovsky works
at his supercomputer, studying the nature of pi.)*

His mother's heart attack
surprised the foreground

one summer weekend, complicating
his search for order,
        the "Deus absconditus"
        in a billion-digit stitch

of fractal landscape. He'd been seeking the spirit
in tides of a wild ratio,

desiring a world of peace
in the mind
        where he might live happily—

the way some of us dream
of a childhood room
        because of its purity
        and abstraction in time.

When there's rain in Chudnovsky mountains
the endless fraction
        unfolds in the mouth of a fish

fooled by surface disturbance, the growing rings
of a pond,

        but now he watches his mother
        closing on death

among the component parts
of his supercomputer
                    that lines the walls

of his apartment. It's a different world
engaging his power
                    when his mouth touches hers

to keep her breathing—then later, plugged
to cyberspace
                    and driving into shapely numbers,

he plays his laptop at the hospital
next to his mother's bed,

watching her blood regain its course
and healthy pressure.

                    Above his coliseum
                    there's a dome of papers

with packed rows of numbers: a steeled
secret code
                    of distant threads, hieroglyphs,

tying it all together. Dreams filter through
most of the time,
                    but weather, always clamorous,
                    comes unbidden.

Brain Mapping

He's getting paid
to lie inside a sterile tube
                    and watch crosshairs

through a helmet, answering nouns
with verbs—

                pure mental activity
                lighting a screen

like squares of cropland
seen from miles up,
                    colored in rates

of flowing blood. But *in medias res*

the map goes wild—lights of a power plant
switching on

with pulses, warnings—like nothing
predicted. Reds and yellows,
                    hundreds, blood

speeding throughout his brain
as if he'd just been born.

They don't believe it and look for errors

but settle on him
as *artifact*—his data
                    impossible to use—

and call the next one in. Having to speak
a single verb
                    in the split second of allotted time,

he couldn't do it. The fraction spilled over
into speechlessness,

                    a confusion
                    of terrible thoughts

crowding his mind, teasing the cortex
and corpus bridge
                    with heated signals—

unmappable
for a reason: too much happened

when he saw the word *families*—flashed
pro forma
                    to each of the subjects—

a quirk of bad timing, a bothersome
coincidence,
                    that his brother had recently died,

revealing to any
interested party
                    the network of life passing.

Perseid

in memory of Henry Sauerwein, 1918-1996

Moods don't matter. We plug them into the arcs,

the flaring roads
>>>>>>>>where impersonal riders
>>>>>>>>are bearing our flags tonight

beyond pettiness
and point of view.
>>>>>>>>Under our backs, alfalfa's a vessel

densely leaved, buoyant, holding us up.

I'm thinking of the white-ink pen
my mother drew across
>>>>>>>>typos and wrong words

when I was a boy watching
the mystery of her work.
>>>>>>>>It's true—much needs to die

or at least get shaped into something else.

The lines are crisp tonight, peremptory,
they do not plead—
>>>>>>>>what we are is getting better.

Circling

*(Although relief missions brought home other, non-Russian members
of the three-person crew aboard the Mir Orbital Platform, Sergei
Krikalev, a Soviet/Russian astronaut, was forced to remain in space
five extra months for budgetary reasons. During this time the Soviet
Union collapsed and Krikalev's hometown was renamed.)*

Even more here, in this "freedom,"
the weightless man

                feels the joints of his bones
                fitted together

for the purpose of force,
the needed leverage
                for daily living—

even more now, the isolation
of a body ill-suited to space
                  and disjunction.

Sometimes he sees a sharp-edged
swath of clouds

when the sun's angle
is long enough, cold enough, on the taiga—

the slow mappings
of dangerous tides
                are touching doorstones.

. . .

To play *the game of seasons*
he puts his mouth near the window

and breathes against his view of Earth.
A circle of fog

           pulls back and vanishes
           with his inward breath:

a speeded replay
of the winter he's lost with family

              whose transparent faces
              begin to wrap the Earth,

adding their forms
to lines of shadow and snow.

       . . .

The wind is up

and countless, flagging stars
pinned to buildings
            at the Baikonur Cosmodrome

resemble red stains
when he pictures them,

              and the patch-symbols
              of his uniform

seem to slip through his body

as though in free fall
and soon to bury themselves.

                    The inboard lights

with their routine demands
for attention—
                pointless, absurd

now their purpose is undermined,
now the good and personal tension
                        of discovery

has narrowed to wires of focus. For whom
has he circled
            four thousand times?

        . . .

Without money
to open it,
        the giant blue door

fixed in a steel
windowless building
            on the Baikonur steppe

      is an inlay
      of vision, a classical

      relic abstracted from use
      on the ice-winded plain . . .

and he's sick of fatigue, of indulging
this form of clarity.

. . .

Reaching him
through static

that's been so much a part of his language:

St. Petersburg, and Lenin is dead officially,
the Earth
            too awfully contingent,

impending, fugitive.

He thinks of driving with his family,
how unseen dust on the windshield

suddenly appears at certain turns,
blurring direction
                    at low sun.

. . .

With atrophied muscles
he'll be unable to rise after landing—

he'll be lifted from his seat
as an invalid

and feel like he's spilling from their hands

on a foreign plain
in Kazakhstan.

. . .

His fingers can spread the window's length.

He's imagined gripping the Earth,
the illusion of a hand-sized ball.

He's imagined swinging
his wife in circles till both

are dizzy and laughing unselfconsciously

among trees coming closer
that sway wave-like on the skyline.

Many lives touch a strip of bark
each spring:

        seeds, birds' feet, his own palm
        the size of a web.

    . . .

Tired of surfaces
that bring to mind

           the reconstruction
           of the arm he'd once broken,

tired of plastic and metal, their chemical
or imagined

smells—
      he wants texture
      that suggests a growing life,

he wants to hold
the length of a wooden ladle

                              and feel the color
                              on tips of fall leaves.

The lines on his palm
are a wild tangle of brush.

                    . . .

When Gagarin returned to Earth

like a signet—
                    the first
                    of his kind, a Soviet,

to orbit the Earth—he was lost,
having fallen

                    from the height of his country's
                    implied threat,

and asked a girl and grandmother
hunting berries in a field

for help, for the miracle
of a nearby phone.

                    . . .

What's the good
of this adventure,

                    its subtle
                    spiritual connection

to everyday struggles, its grandeur

suggesting the soul's portion
of living—

          that borderless
          sensibility—

if consumers dictate the balance,

if they can't help
but plead

          to the hierarchy
          of empty shelves,

the only world, the near one,
that matters?

          . . .

He's reassured
by personal history,

how the numberless, lived flavors of the past—

like their families
starting as one

when a frozen branch cracked, just missing
their apartment—

will blend with changes
and ease adjustment,

or the way his child's
funny syllables

        seem close to words
        as they come over the radio

like openwork of water
           left behind
           when white-fronted geese

take off. Resemblance
          manages the distance
          between them.